Marian Wolters

ROLF HARTUNG **Creative Textile Design**

Thread and Fabric

 NEW YORK **Reinhold Publishing Corporation**

© Otto Maier Verlag, Ravensburg, Germany, 1963

Published in the United States of America, 1964
By Reinhold Publishing Corporation
Library of Congress Catalog Card No. 64-13650
Printed in Holland

Thread is the source of all textile material. In the form of twine, yarn, line, string, cord, rope or cable, it has always stirred man's creative urge. Spinning, weaving, knotting and knitting are age-old crafts. That is why, even today, the making of something out of thread can be a most valuable addition to our education—an education which tends in this technological age to place an excessive value on intellect and technical ability.

We often use 'thread' and other kindred words in figures of speech. If something has worn thin through frequent repetition we call it 'threadbare'; we follow the 'thread' of an argument; we 'spin a yarn'. Such figures of speech—linking a technical process and a creative act—clearly show how aptly thread lends itself to creative play.

The various ways shown us by Rolf Hartung, in which we can play with thread, awaken memories of childhood, when our actions still lacked 'utility' and so led us towards imaginative creation. But in this book we also see the methods by which, whether young or old, talented or not, we can recapture our original creative powers through play, and how we can meaningfully apply them.

It is the special aim of this book to introduce the reader to a game played according to certain rules. It is not intended to give technical instructions, but to show some of the many possibilities there are in creative play. That is why the illustrations are not meant to be copied; they are meant to encourage us to use the same methods and to achieve similar results. We get to know the technical processes by our own trial and error, and thus gain a direct understanding of textile products, whether hand-made or factory-made.

More important than the results is the liberation achieved by practical work—work which is not based on previous knowledge but which finds expression and fulfilment in creative play.

Ernst Röttger

CONTENTS

In illustrations of children's work, B denotes boys and G denotes girls; these symbols are followed by the age of the child.

The translator, Mr Brian Battershaw, and the publishers are most grateful to Mr Kenneth E. Carlson, to the German Naval Attaché in London, and to the Boys Scouts' Association for advice on various technical points in this book.

Thread and textile fabrics are so available to us that we tend to take them for granted. It is largely by means of the vast variety of woven, knotted and knitted textiles that we fashion our immediate environment. Textiles afford man protection and security, while the choice and combination of materials according to texture and color underlines the individual character of the wearer.

Through the production of textiles, it became possible for man to escape from the confines of a limited climatic region, to penetrate territories that had hitherto been too inhospitable, to extend his living space, and to become mobile and active on a grand scale.

At one time, men were compelled to manufacture textiles for themselves, and so were familiar with both the raw materials and the process of fabrication; the rules of the craft were handed down from generation to generation for thousands of years. Such familiarity has now almost completely vanished. This is the age of the machine and of the specialist; the production of textiles has been taken over by the textile industry, and we are spared the necessity of engaging in it ourselves. Yet there remains a close bond between man and thread and all that is woven from thread. If we accept the fact that man is in this strange and almost magical manner bound up with these things, it seems natural enough that in his play with the materials he should become aware of the timeless principles involved and find his way anew towards certain basic forms and towards certain basic understandings.

PLAY

It is of the essence of play that it should take place under certain limitations. These limitations are provided by the rules. It is only by obeying them that we can come to terms with the game, and can penetrate more and more deeply into a subject matter whose inherent principles all the players must accept. Free acceptance of this obligation to obey the rules opens up a multitude of ways of play. The player of his own accord discovers the manner of fashioning his play that is best suited to him.

In this creative play in which we engage, the experience of the creative process is more important than the result. In solving problems through play there exists something that is liberating and important, something to which all attempts to attain an objective visualized in advance and to follow a prescribed plan are definitely hostile. The objective reveals itself and impresses itself all the more effectively upon our minds, the more freely and naturally we move towards it by way of play. The end-product therefore should come into being unfettered by any notion of utility.

If we compare the various forms created through play and seek to find out what they express, we attain an enhanced capacity for self-criticism and an enhanced understanding of the character of other people. We become conscious of our play-experience and there is a refinement of our feeling for form.

MATERIALS

Very many primary materials are used today in the production of textiles. For our purpose let us for the moment choose those derived from vegetable fiber. The method of processing them has been known for many years. The wood and stalk parts of the plants are removed. The network of fibers is laid bare, and is divided up, along with the comb-like hackle, first into single fibers and then into fibers lying next to each other in strands. Because of their rough surface, the fibers hold together quite easily by means of small pieces that have been torn away and are left sticking out. The fibers get wedged and hooked on to each other and can be fitted together in any length we please. Linen fibers are soft. Hemp is both firmer and rougher and is used for the manufacture of string, cord and rope. Sometimes sisal, a stiff bulky fiber, is mixed with coarser Manilla hemp and short-fibered jute. This changes the make-up of string very slightly, and account should be taken of it.

To carry on the game we require the following: a strand of hemp, which we call oakum; a short-fibered soft hempen thread; string of various strengths; and cord of simple and multiple twining made from long hempen fibers. We also need sacking of various colors as well as natural; this is woven from jute. In addition we need linen of not too fine a texture. In certain jobs it is advisable to use sandpaper and emery paper as a backing. Textile colors soluble in water should be used for coloring.

TOOLS

Though we need scissors to cut the thread, the universal tool for everything we make is our hands. Other aids and specialized tools are not required. They weaken the direct experience that comes to us in play. The activity of our hands is of decisive importance for the way our play develops. They are at one and the same time an organ of experience and an executive instrument. The perceptible stimulus which thread and woven matter give to the touch of the fingers sets the hands purposefully in motion by the speediest of reflexes. Its inclusion in the creative process has a therapeutic effect and brings about a relaxing of tension in the player. A thing that is known by touch is of necessity a thing close at hand; it inspires confidence and this leads to its 'intelligibility'. The activity of the hands sets up a kind of sympathetic rhythm that affects the whole man. The union of tactile and visual experience gives impressions a more solid and durable character, and the power of expression is thus enhanced. Textile media are experienced, as it were, from several points of view. They are thus able to act upon us in a manner that is all the more impressive and convincing.

BASIC RULES

1. All games played with thread must be carried out with the hands alone and without any other aid.
2. The material consists of threads and of textiles made of plant fiber.
3. The tasks accomplished must not be thought of as serving any useful purpose.

The creative means consists of the actual character of the material and the corresponding methods of work upon it. Design elements such as the dot, the line, the spot and the surface will appear in the form of the knot, the thread and woven fabric. By winding, stretching and encircling, it is possible to call into being plastic forms of spatial extension and with both hollow and convex portions. With all the tasks set, an effort is made to use these creative means to achieve a certain order. The limited means employed causes the fashioning of the image to be impressive and makes what it has to tell us clearly articulate. Here too limitation brings about an increase in depth.

The first two sections deal with the characteristics of thread and with certain basic principles of handicraft which must be observed. Each of the other sections is independent in itself and can be played in any order. Within each of these areas there can grow up an understanding of the whole. From the examples in the illustrations we can recognize the various methods of play. The rules which apply in each case can be clearly discerned. The illustrations are intended to serve as incentives to join in the game and to suggest a number of further variations. A number of the examples lead us on to textile techniques. Here playing with thread may help us to grasp certain connections and may prove a useful starting point for the study of technical procedures. The understandings that we have gained in play will remain valid and effective even in a wider field.

Hemp fibers are the primary material for the production of thread. The string used in our play is made of short fibers, cord and rope out of long and more durable fibers.

1

If we try to twist a complete strand of hempen fibers together, it will not remain in its new state. Only a small quantity of fibers (2) can be twisted together into a thread (3). Their surface attachment to each other must be stronger than their elasticity. Damp lessens the tension of the fiber. When being twisted, the fibers should be held in one hand and twisted in one direction with the thumb and forefinger of the other. Later the other hand can strengthen the effect of the twist by twisting in the opposite direction. The act of producing a hempen thread by our own efforts is one that leaves a distinct impression upon us. If a thread is twisted beyond the adhesive power of the fibers, then it unwinds itself when we let go of it. If an overtwisted thread is held at each end and bent together, both parts of the thread will wind themselves about each other in a spiral (4).

2   3   4

11

5

A comparatively strong machine-made piece of string has been unraveled (5). It is plain that it was produced from a number of threads and twisted in the opposite direction to that of the individual threads. The playful unraveling of the thread itself leads to certain results of a personal kind. The hempen fibers of a piece of string that has been unraveled have been laid next to one another (6). The fibers do not smooth themselves out, they still adhere to each other and retain some remnant of the twist. From these partly plucked-out threads we obtain groups and rows of large and small spindle forms. The contrast between the firm, linear elements and those that are looser and have the character of extended surfaces governs the order in which the threads are placed in relation to one another.

6

13

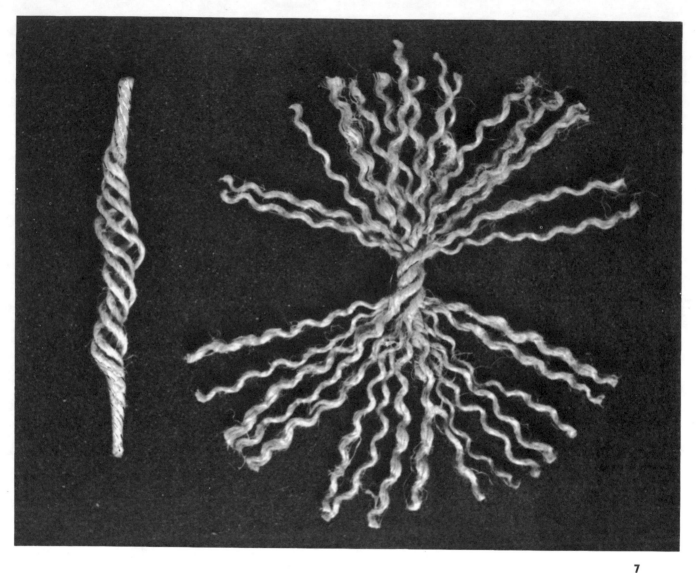

7

If placed on emery paper, the threads need only slight pressure to make them adhere to the rough surface. By removing and replacing them, we can in the course of our play make a number of pictorial arrangements, without depriving the whole of the freshness and spontaneity of its message.

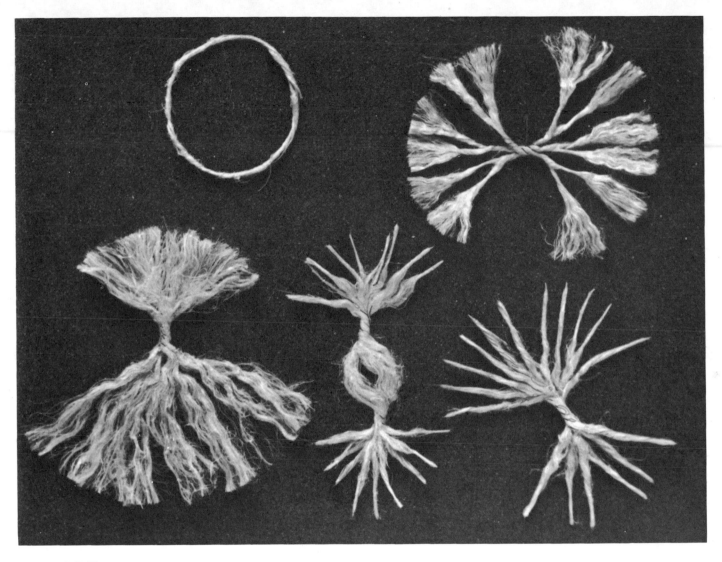

8 G 17

Both ends of the threads are twisted open and branch out. In two of the shapes (bottom right and center) the ends of the fibers are twisted together again afresh. The ring (top left) shows how the fibers hook smoothly into each other without any break in the line.

9

The way the threads twist and unravel themselves makes us realize that thread comes into being as the result of a twisting pressure which the fibers unwillingly obey. This struggle between the two forces remains hidden, but produces the characteristic behaviour of the loose thread.

16

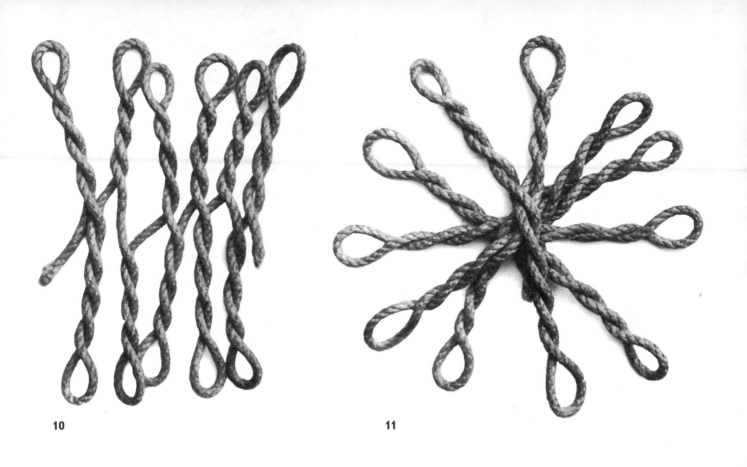

10   11

The overtwisting of a thread (4) is resorted to in the row of loops (10) and in the loop-star (11). This shows clearly how the properties of the material determine the use by the player of the means at his disposal. Play with the material leads to the discovery of the processes best adapted to it.

17

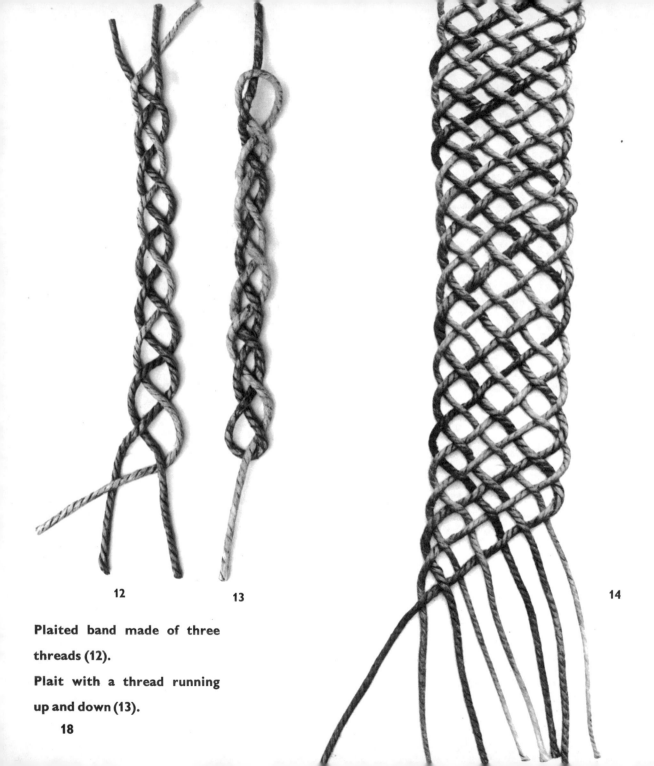

12 **13** **14**

Plaited band made of three
threads (12).
Plait with a thread running
up and down (13).

18

15 B 12

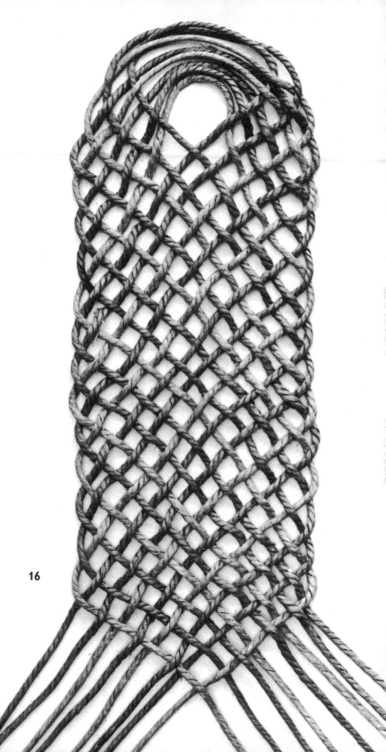

16

Plaited spiral (15).

In the narrow plaited bands (12, 13) the single thread, because of its curving line, still acts as an independent partner. The broader the band becomes, the more a new process comes into being: namely the passing over and underneath one another of the threads, which in their wave-shaped line hold each other in place and form the plaiting. This is particularly clear in one example (14) where eight and in another (16) where sixteen threads are plaited together.

17   18

Fourfold plaiting (18) is shown in its separate phases in Figure 17. The second and fourth threads are always laid across the first and third, then the first crosses the third. It is easy in plaiting to combine four-threaded bands at right angles to each other (19). This makes plain the relation between plaiting and weaving.

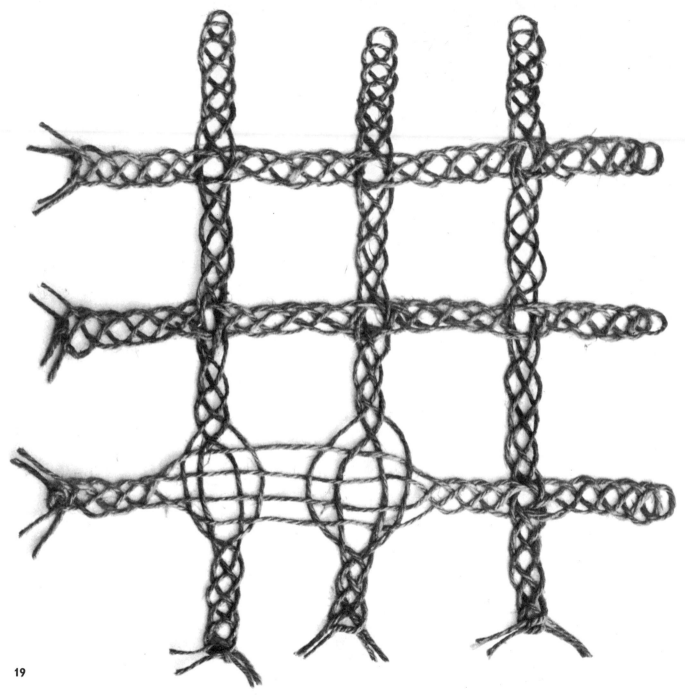

19

21

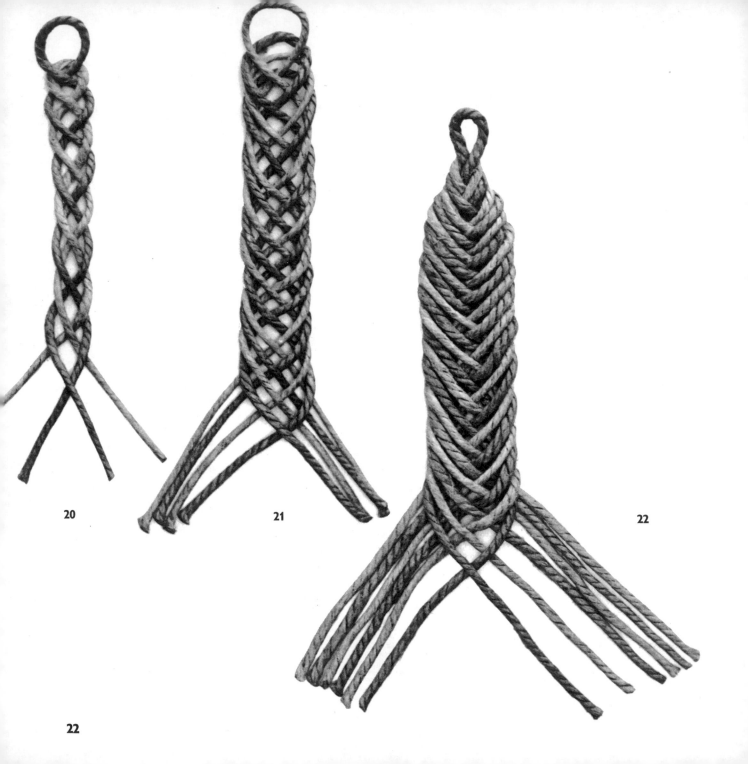

20

21

22

22

The 'Chinese pigtail' allows threads to be continuously added. The threads are hung in from behind in the form of a simple loop. The plaiting process itself is simple. The outer threads are laid crossing one another into the open center (20, 21, 22). Colored threads make it easier to take the whole pattern in at a glance. The ends that stick out obliquely can be combined with other pigtails, as the pigtail plaiting shows (23).

23

24

25

With interplaiting, the threads increase in firmness. The breadth of the plaited bands is, however, limited by the pull at the edges and the difficulty of keeping the whole pattern in view where many threads are employed. It is simpler to add strength by twisting threads together into cords and ropes. Here the roundness remains and with it the all-round mobility. In making firm the end of a rope we can obtain a circular plaiting (24,25). In the plaiting knot (27) a plaiting corresponding to Figure 24 has been attempted from the rope. In forming the loop (28) and also in Figure 26 the ends have been reversed and plaited between the cords of the rope, which have been loosened for this purpose (splicing).

24

26

27

28

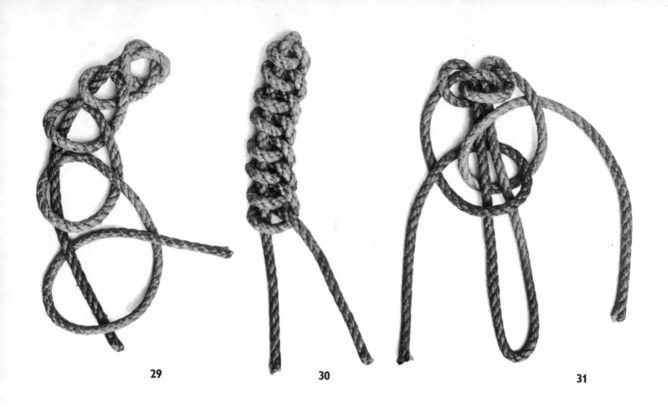

29   30   31

The dark end of the thread is laced about with a half knot: the 'half-hitch' (29). A number of such hitches have been pushed together on the main thread (30). The 'eight' is loosely drawn together and the guide thread remains visible. If the guide thread is drawn taut, the result is a firm but not very flexible configuration: the 'spiral stair' of thread (33). The half-hitches arrange themselves in a spiral sequence around the inner thread. The half-hitches are laid alternately from either side around the main thread which is laid out to form a loop (31). As you press the half-hitches together you get the 'string-tongue' which can be turned screw-fashion in both directions (34).

26

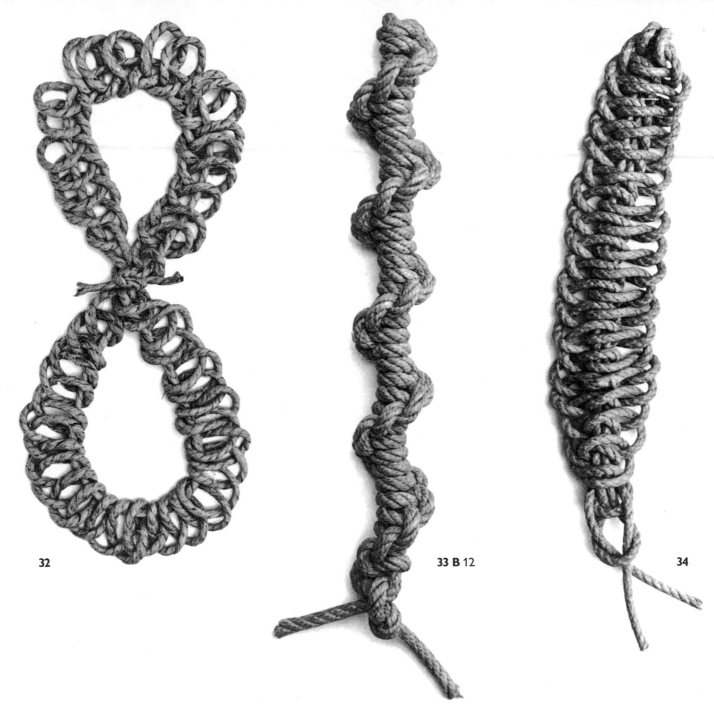

32   33 B 12   34

27

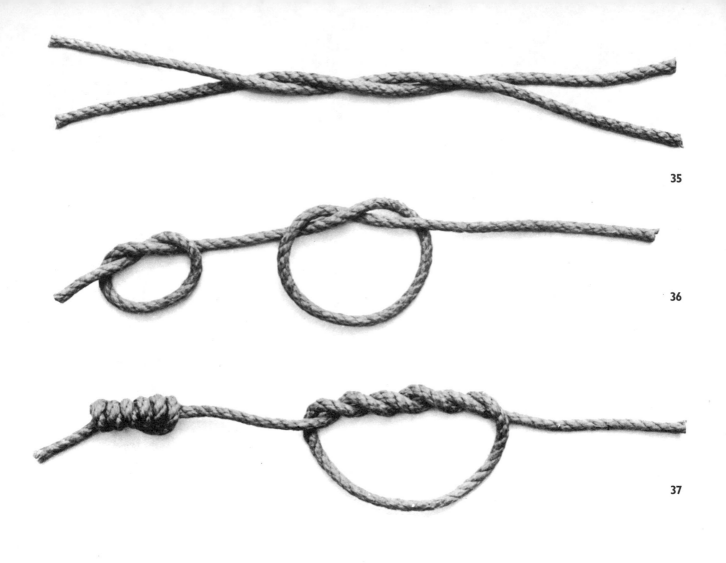

35

36

37

A knot is formed; the two ends of a thread are laid over each other so as to form a loop (36). The principle of the spiral winding of thread and string also finds its application in the knot.

28

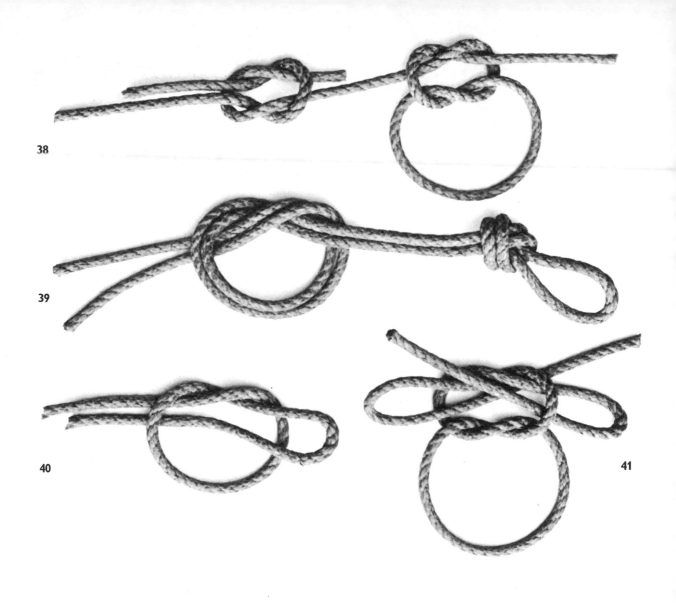

In the tailor's knot the string is wound several times about itself (37). The reef knot (38) consists of two knots that lie opposite each other. The two-threaded loop knot (39), the disappearing loop knot (40) and the combined slip knot, are all different forms of knots. We use knots to join threads together and to strengthen their ends.

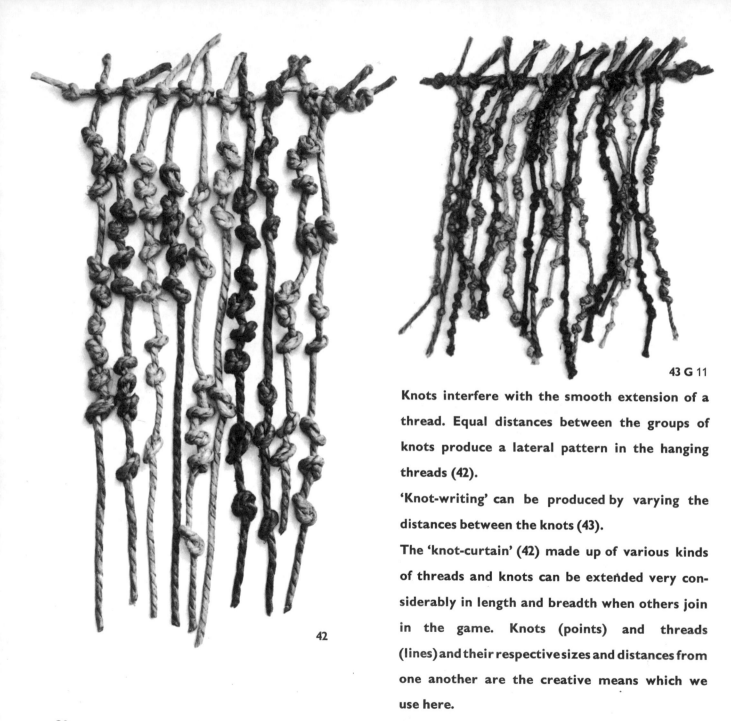

43 G 11

42

Knots interfere with the smooth extension of a thread. Equal distances between the groups of knots produce a lateral pattern in the hanging threads (42).

'Knot-writing' can be produced by varying the distances between the knots (43).

The 'knot-curtain' (42) made up of various kinds of threads and knots can be extended very considerably in length and breadth when others join in the game. Knots (points) and threads (lines) and their respective sizes and distances from one another are the creative means which we use here.

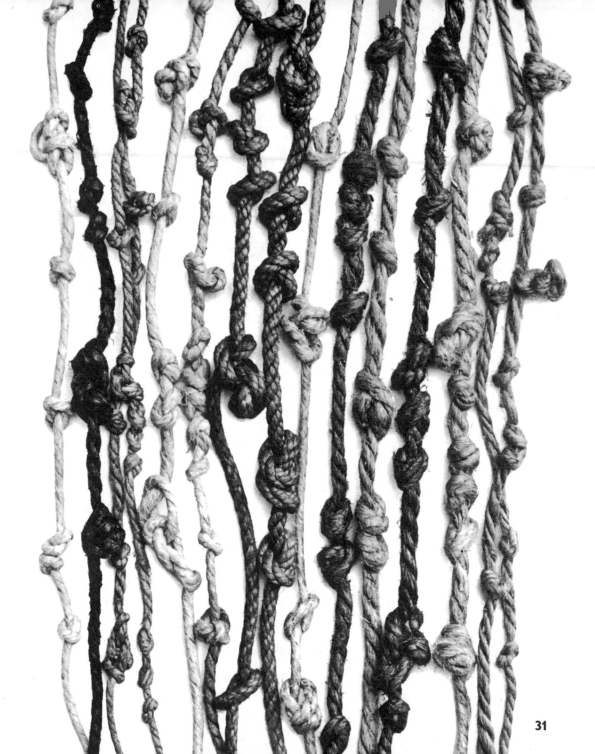

44 G 18

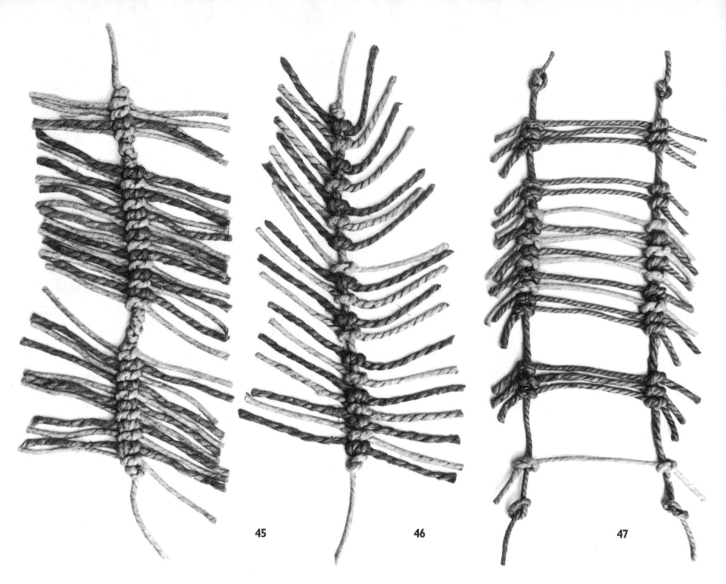

45 46 47

Short threads are knotted onto a longer main thread. The free ends stick out obliquely, depending on the position of the threads in the knots. By varying the knots (right over left or vice versa) the ends can be made to stick out in opposite directions. Figure 47 shows a 'thread-ladder'.

In 46 and 48, the ends of the threads have been twisted in a different direction from their original one, to produce a V-shaped arrangement.

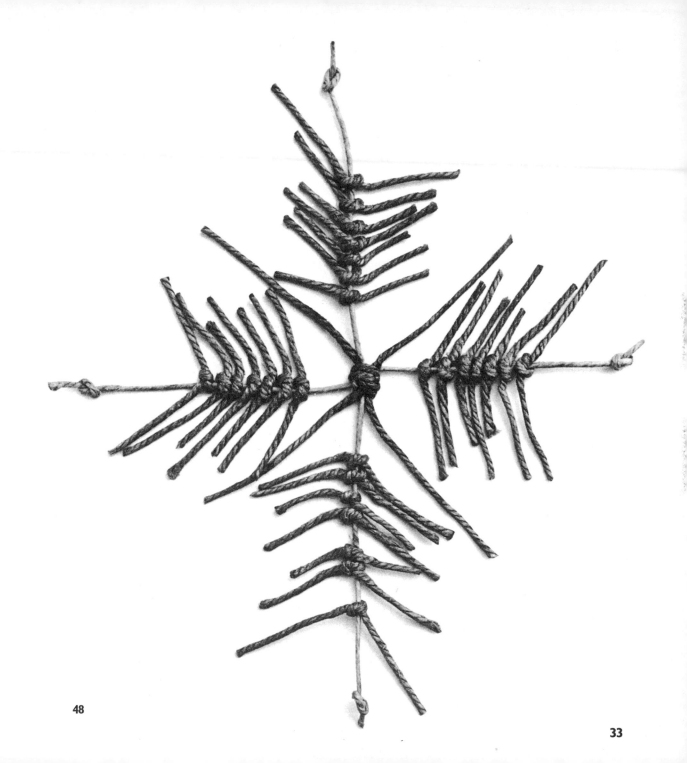

48

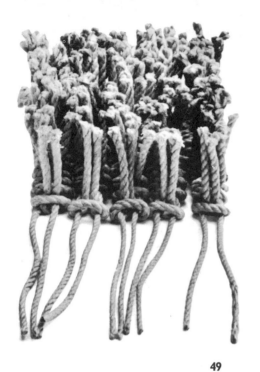

49

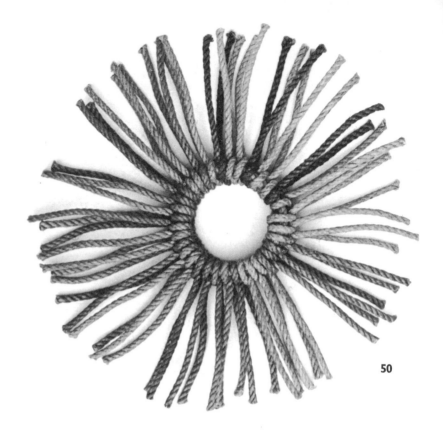

50

51

An open knot formation (51) is called a Smyrna knot. If the thread which is to be worked into the pattern (53) is hung into pairs of the cord, the result is a carpet or a brush (49). After every row of Smyrna knots, cross threads are tied to counteract a tendency to crookedness and to ensure greater firmness. If the desired length is not attained, the pairs of cords are knotted. Many knotting and weaving techniques are based on the Smyrna knot.

34

52 **G** 17

Because of their wedge-like shape, Smyrna knots worked into a pair of cords, form a circle (50). The 'centipede' (52) gets its curved shape through changing the knots worked in. Straight parts are obtained by counter-knots and by winding the thread around. If the ends of the Smyrna knots are not too long, then their number makes the centipede stand up (hempen cord).

53

The loop forms the basis for a number of textile techniques, such as crochet work and knitting. In contrast to woven material, knitted articles are made of a single long thread. Every loop or mesh holds the one next to it and if one breaks, the whole of the work disintegrates.

Into the knot at the beginning of the thread we draw the first loop (54). Through it the next one is stuck and so on (55). Each time this process of sticking through has been completed, the previous loop is pulled taut. Such a chain of loops is like the beginning of crochet work (57).

If we stitch loops with two threads (56) we get a narrow firm band. Four such crossing threads give us a plastic formation with a rhythmic pattern, which looks rather like a natural object—children call it a 'corn cob' (59).

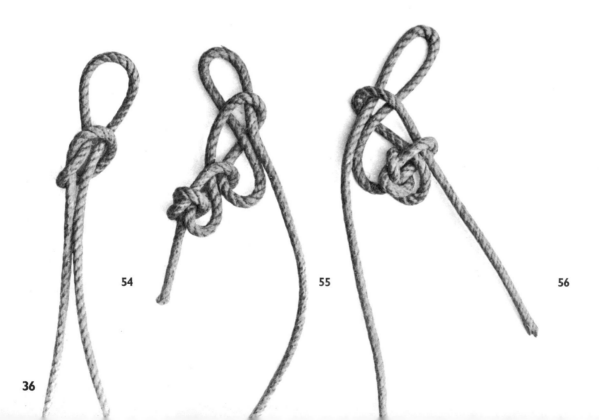

54   55   56

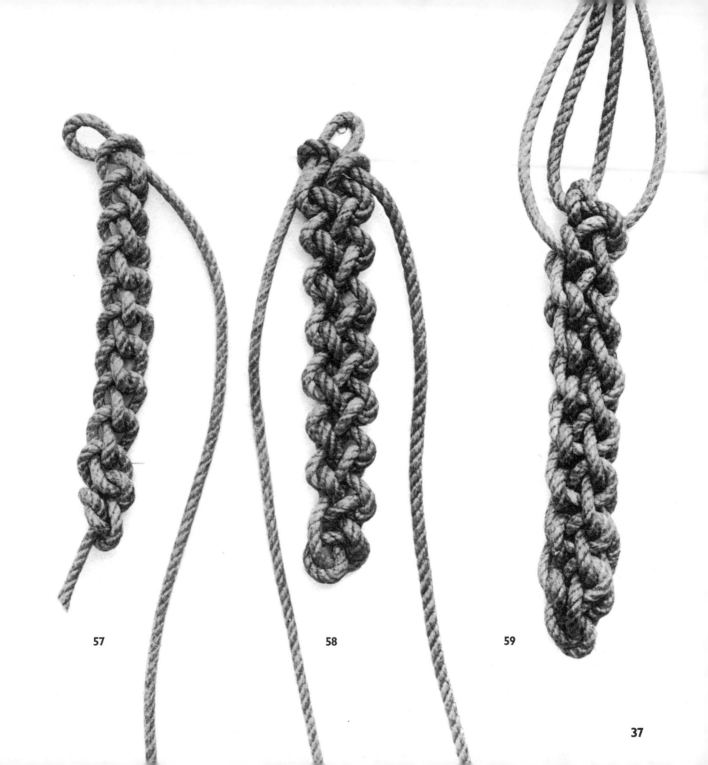

57   58   59

37

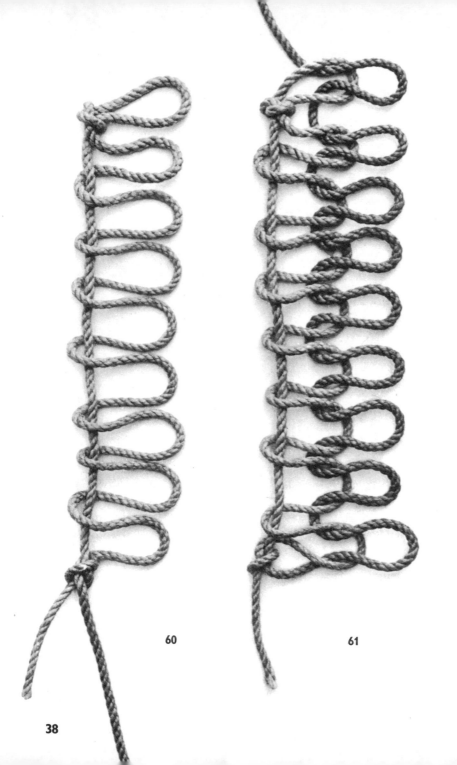

60

61

A series of adjacent loops becomes a kind of wave formation (60). The same thread is then reversed and a further series of loops completed (61). In this knitting without needles, row can be added to row and hard mats (62) or soft pliable bits of knitting can be produced, the result depending on the size of the loops and the material used. Admittedly the choice of color and material, the density of the knitting and the size of the object are matters of personal choice, but the chief value of the activity is in its rhythmic repetition and the harmonious resolution of tensions it achieves.

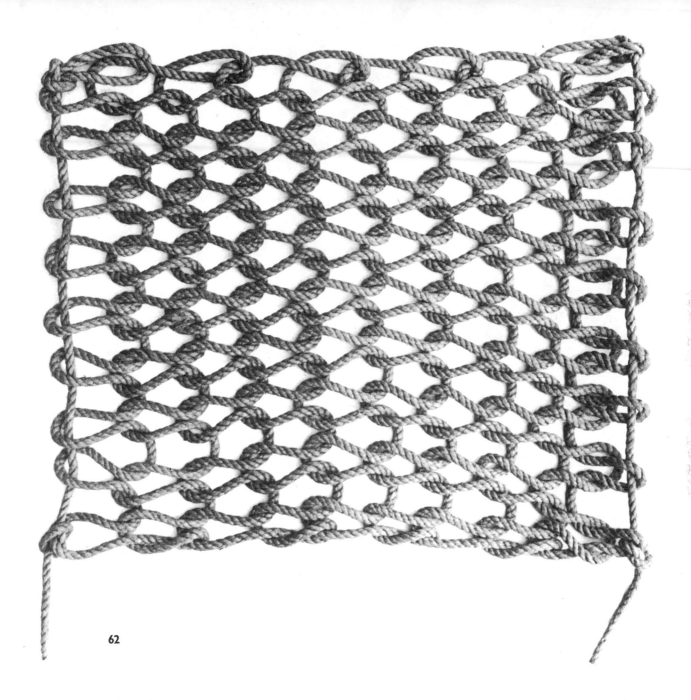

62

Mat with two-color thread.

63 **G** 12

40

64

The somewhat unstable formation of loop knots (64) requires some object on which they can be made firm—another loop or another thread. In Figures 63 and 65 hard bulky sisal thread has been used for this purpose. By drawing the loops tight the sisal thread is held firm. The winding of the chain of loops is very evident in the form attained (63). Parallel chains of loops prevent such winding (65). In both cases the possibilities inherent in the material and in the method of treating it have been skilfully exploited. Opportunities of relating the forms to known objects as in the 'rope-ladder' and the 'thread-caterpillar' will come to mind after the play has created the forms. An object should not be regarded at the outset as the purpose of the work.

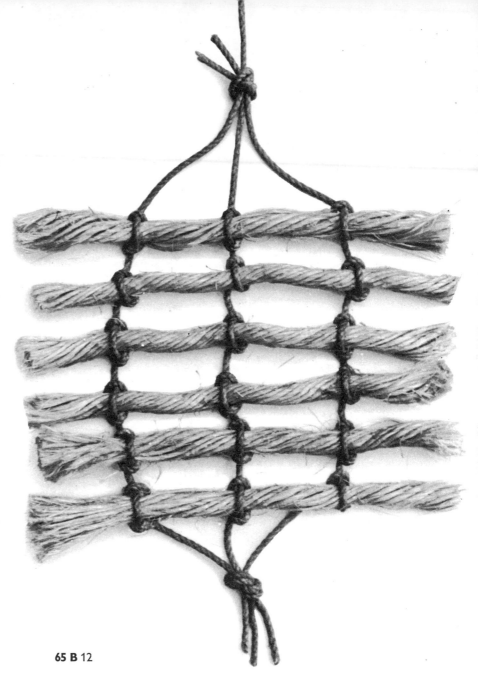

65 B 12

41

42

66   67   68

The single thread does not have much body. Its length is excessive compared with its thickness. It acquires more body if one or more threads are wound around it. Figure 66 shows wrapping round a cord with a winding thread that alternates between close and loose winding. Changes in the line of the base cord should be held fast by winding another cord around it (67). Total and individual windings may be made round a number of cords (68).

In Figure 69 the slender mobile base cord which can be seen above and below becomes a full oval pendulum by having many threads wrapped around it. By continually changing the direction of the windings we get a 'ball-pendulum' (70). Such pendulums are useful preliminary exercises for the mobile thread marionettes which follow.

69

70

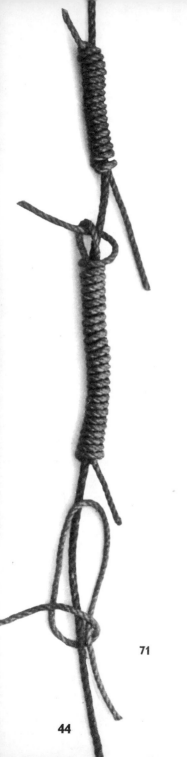

72

71

44

As Figure 71 (below) shows, the base cord has a loop from another cord laid upon it, and base cord and loop are thickly wound about from the bottom of the loop till only a small eye remains free at the very top. Through this eye there is drawn the cord that does the winding (71 middle). If the beginning of the loop is now pulled, then the winding becomes firm on the cord beneath (71 above). It is called a 'coil'.

Such a coil has many uses. It can hold many threads together or can be laid around a single thread. It can also only be wound around a loop. If such a single-thread coil is bent in the shape of a circle and the beginning and end of the cord are drawn together through the eye of the loop, the result is the 'coil-ring' (72).

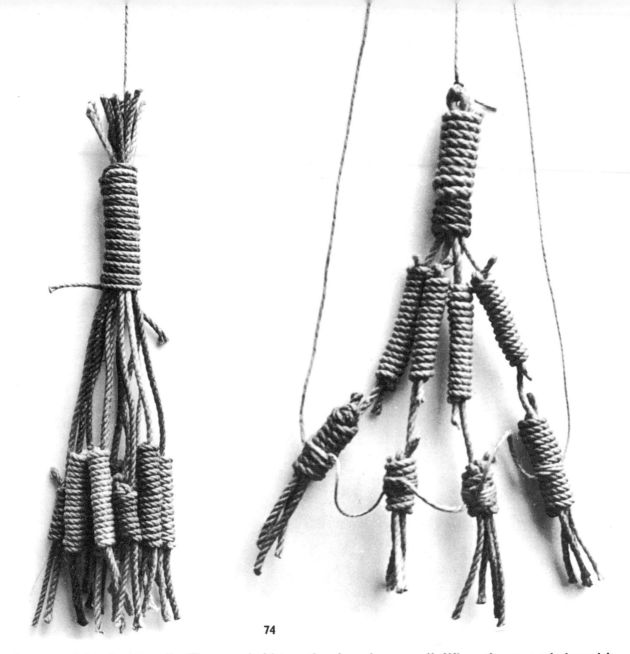

73　　　　　　　　**74**

Hempen cords are weighted with coils. They are held together by a larger coil. When the central thread is turned, the hanging coils whirl apart (73). The articulated coil figure (74) can be moved in a fan-like fashion by its guide cords.

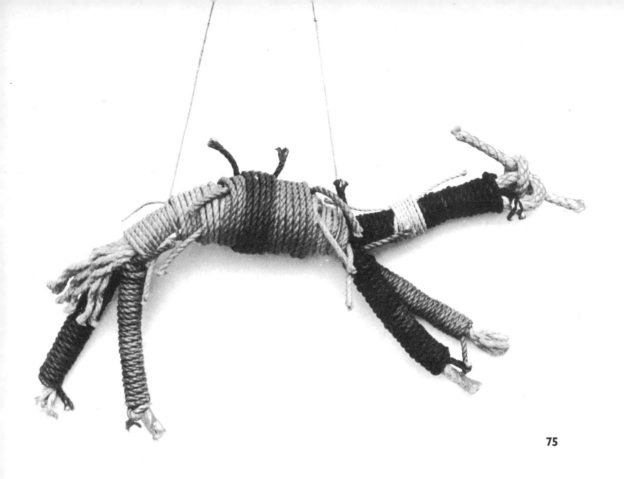

75

The hanging coil figures (75, 76, 77, 78), have been fixed onto the same framework of cords. This involves two loops of cord being laid upon one another pointing in opposite directions. One loop forms the head while its ends form the legs; the other loop forms the rear and the ends the arms. The mobility of the limbs depends on whether the coils have been partially or completely wound around the ends of the cords. If equipped with guiding threads, the figures become thread-marionettes.

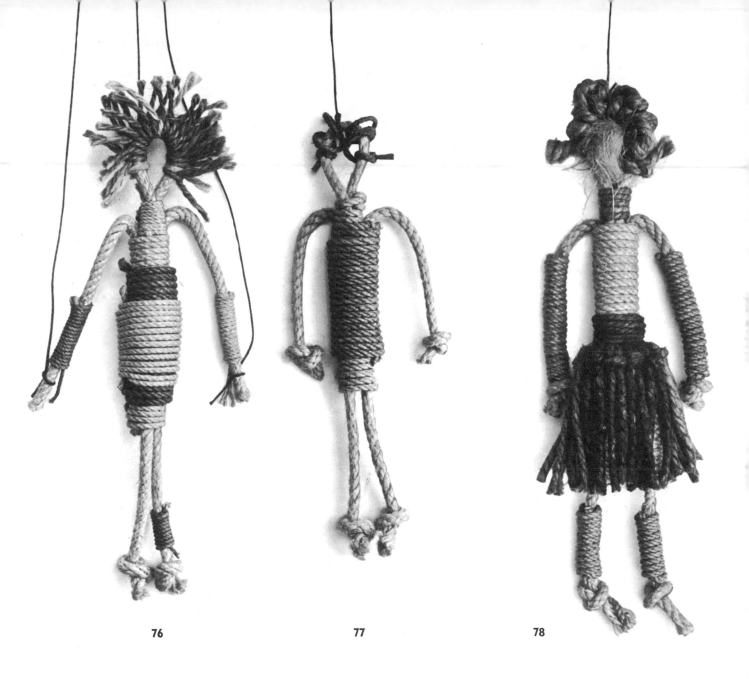

76

77

78

79

For standing figures sisal cord, which is quite stiff, will be found useful. The sisal framework of the lion (79) was wrapped around with coconut cord. The soft mane has been laid on with hempen fiber.

When hanging shapes are made, the force of gravity counteracts the thread's flexibility. By tying together bundles of thread we get tassels (Plate 1, opp. page 48). Their length is best determined by the measure of one's hand. The thread is wound round the hand, tied together and cut open on one or both sides (hempen yarn). If firmer threads are used, a similar procedure can be employed to produce transparent figures. Thin hempen cords are fastened to a central thread by means of coils. If we shorten the central thread, the hempen cords are pushed outwards and make a more convex shape. Shapes are formed which enclose space but through which we can see. The degree of transparency is affected by the number and color of the threads. The varying distances between the coils determine the size and number of the thread-balls. These light and merry thread-signals move with every breath of wind (81).

In Figure 82 the space from the center outwards is taken up by the ends of the threads which are knotted in such a way as to form a spiral around the main thread. In Figure 83 a shape that encloses a space is formed by the tying-in of circular threads.

81 G 18

The camel was plaited out of coconut fiber. Coils of string hold the ends together.

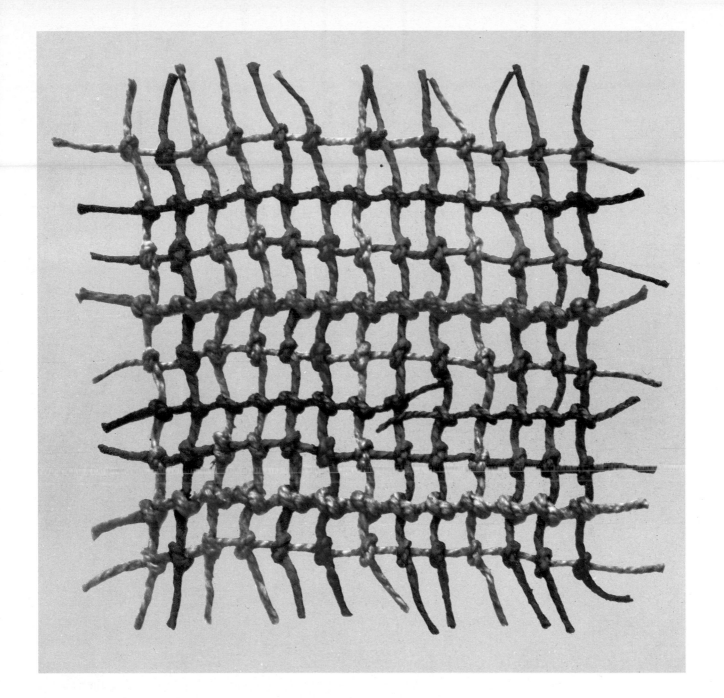

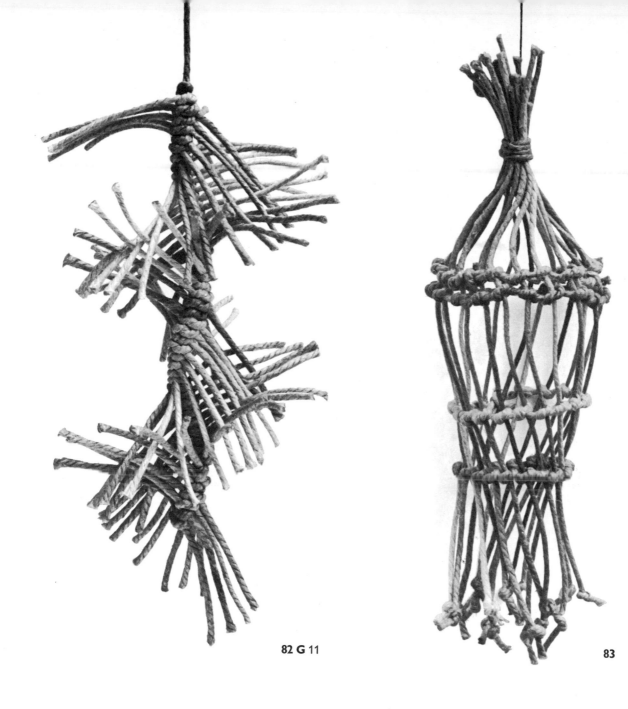

82 G 11

83

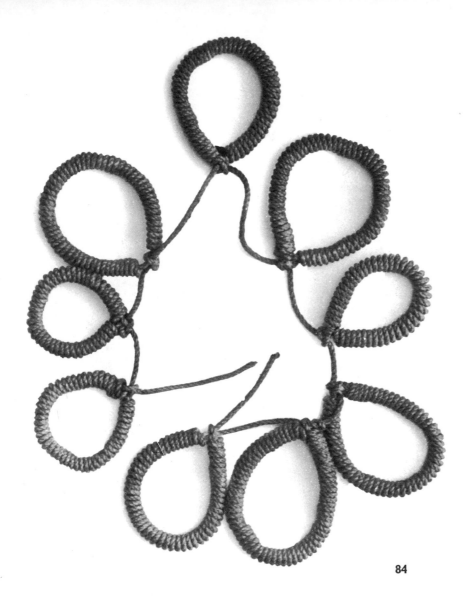

84

Coil-rings of varying size are fixed one after the other on to a long cord, producing a 'garland of rings' (84). Coil-rings of colored cord are connected with each other at the ends of the threads by coils (85). The diagonal movement of the lines of the threads as they are drawn across each other is in lively contrast to the closed circular forms. The rings and the many points of connection hold the 'net-chain' securely together.

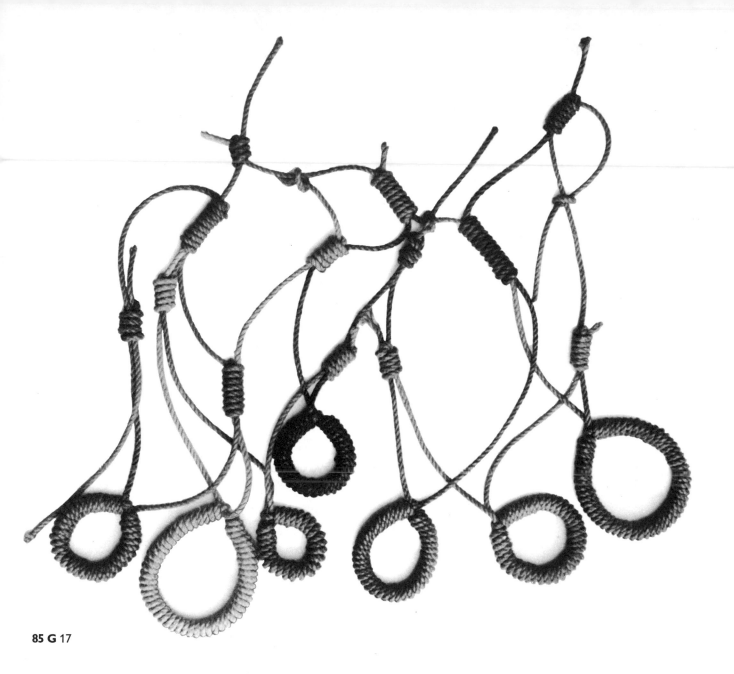

85 G 17

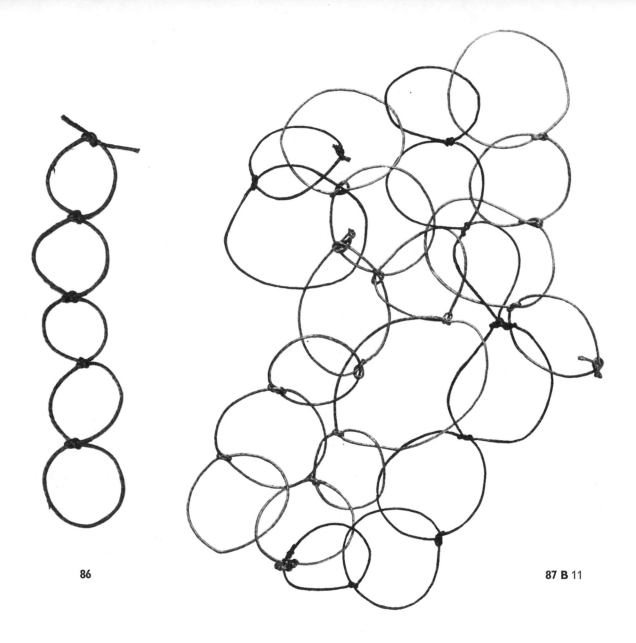

86

87 B 11

The threads are tied together by means of a cross-knot and so form circles, ultimately producing a chain of circular links (86).

A net of interlocking circular meshes is made from a number of pieces of string (87).

54

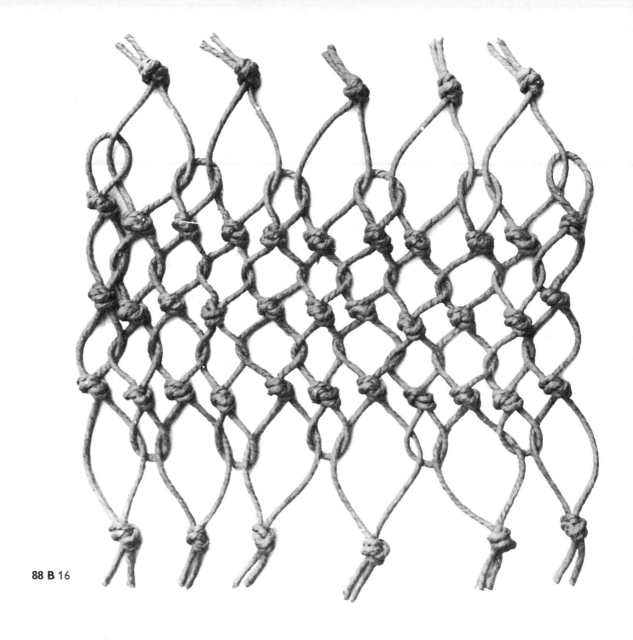

88 **B** 16

The rows of meshes of the net-band (88) have been fastened with the firm fisherman's knot. The rows consist of three small meshes and a large one. The rows are hung into each other from opposite directions. The general effect is that of a horizontal band.

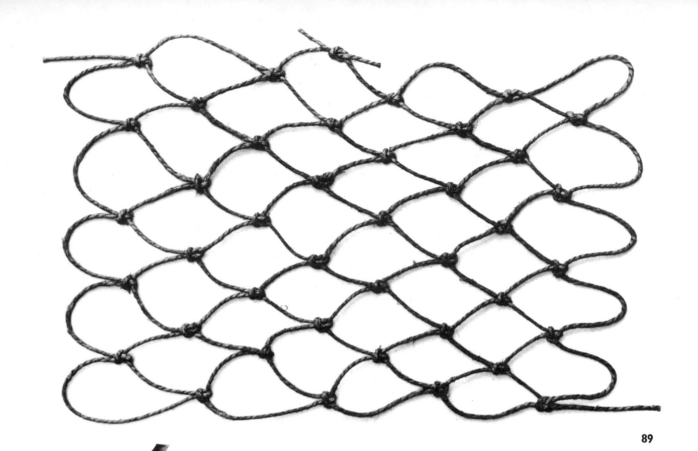

89

90

Nets are produced by knotting threads into meshes. It is the function of a net both to let through and to prevent from going through.

The fisherman's net (89) is knotted with the bowline knot (90) which when drawn tightly is particularly secure. The meshes in the first row which were originally round are drawn into rhomboid shape by having other meshes worked into them. The meshes lie next to each other honeycomb-fashion in the net. When the net is stretched from all sides, the meshes become square-shaped.

91

Part of a net made from colored hempen twine with ring tassels.

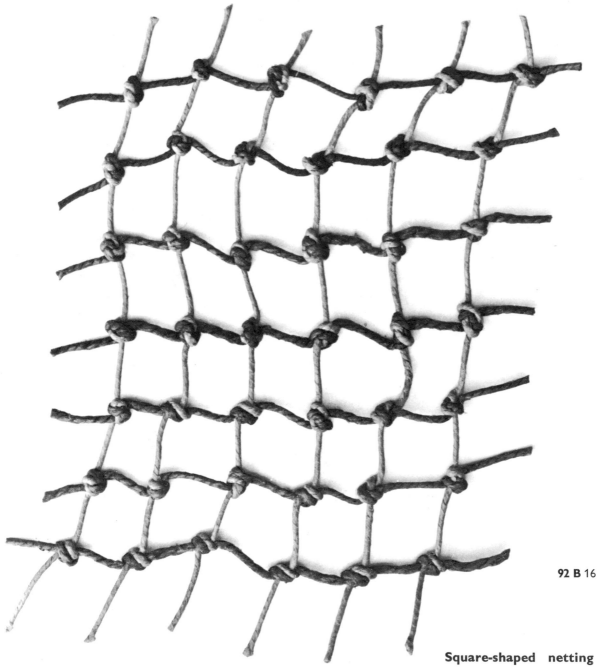

92 B 16

Square-shaped netting with fisherman's knots. See also Plate II.

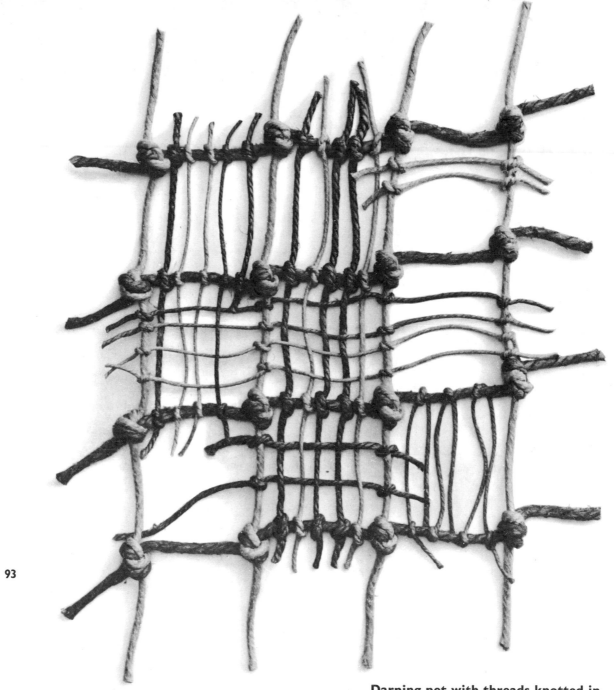

93

Darning net with threads knotted in.

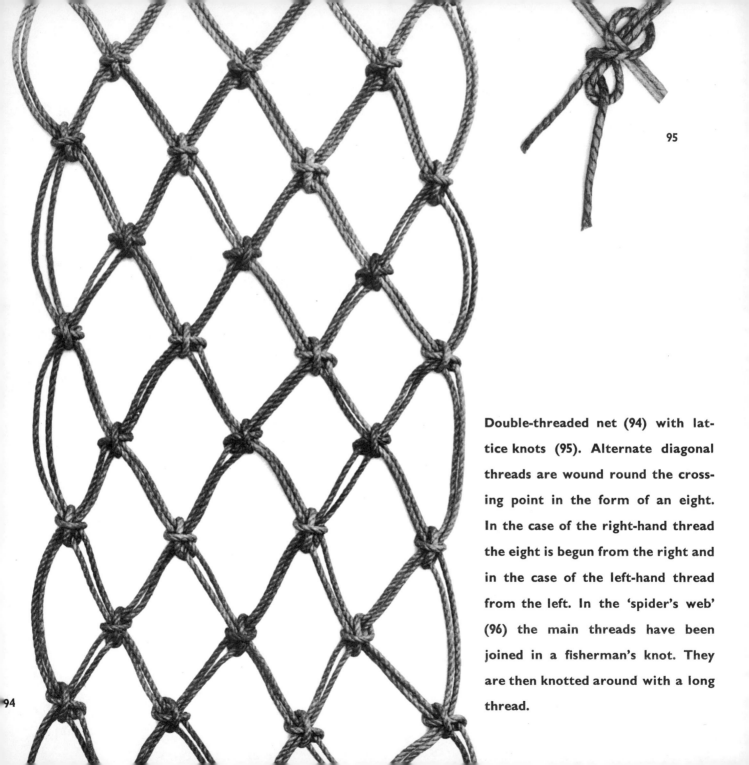

95

Double-threaded net (94) with lattice knots (95). Alternate diagonal threads are wound round the crossing point in the form of an eight. In the case of the right-hand thread the eight is begun from the right and in the case of the left-hand thread from the left. In the 'spider's web' (96) the main threads have been joined in a fisherman's knot. They are then knotted around with a long thread.

94

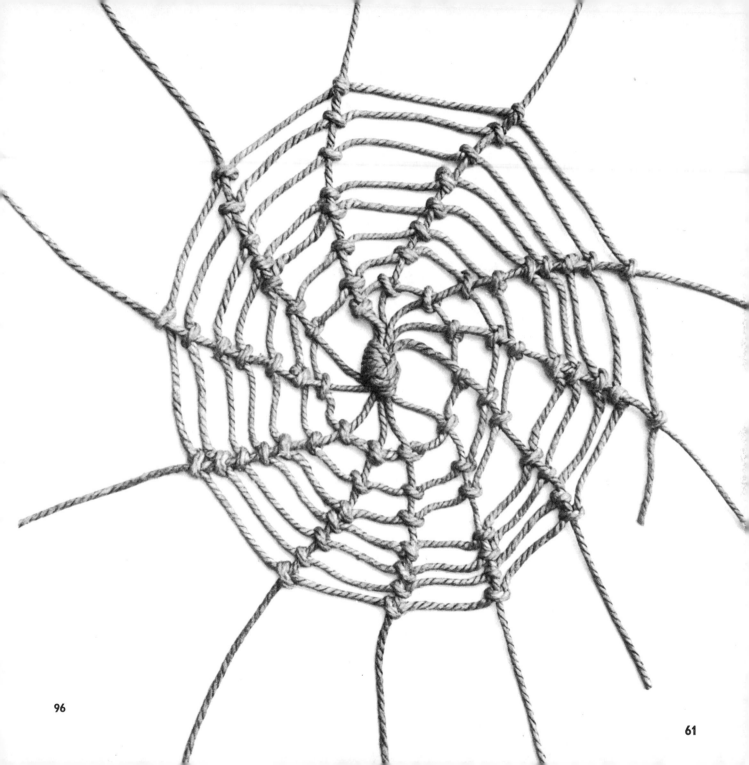

96

61

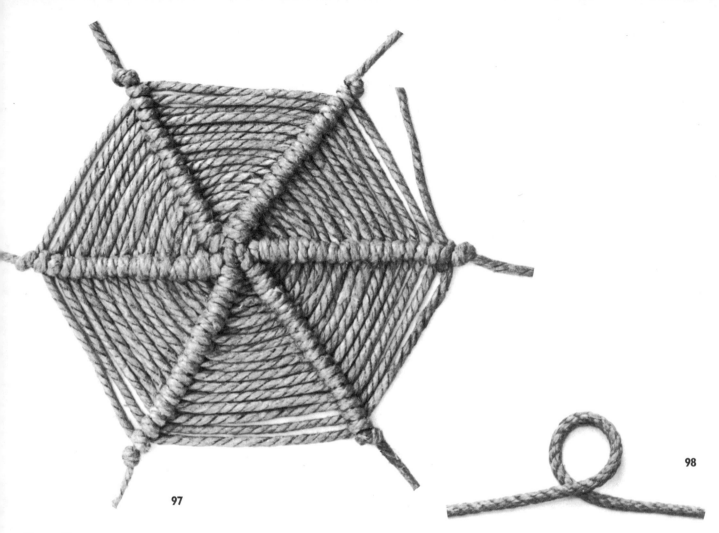

97

98

From the center a cord is wound around three cords that cross each other, each of these cords being held in a half-bend (98). The half-bends are themselves held fast by knots at the ends. Thus we can made a 'thread-hexagon' (97).

In the winding-round (99), the hempen threads have been knotted in close formation around the inner ring of strong cord. Further, the cord is laid in a spiral while at the same time the hempen threads are drawn over and under the cord. Thus a firmly fashioned plate of cord is obtained which grows out from the center. New threads can be continually hooked in.

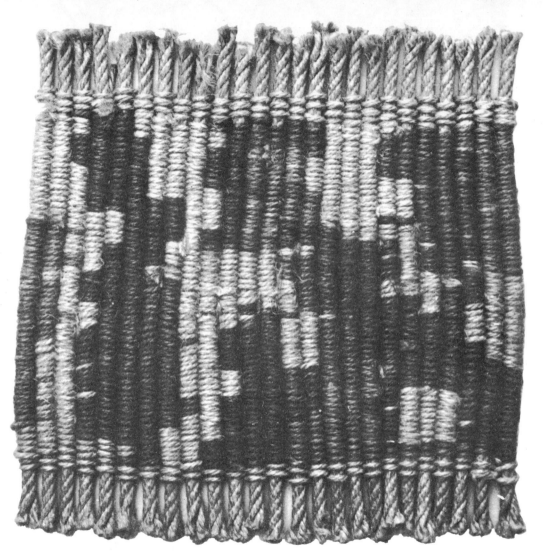

100

101 G 17

Cords lying next to one another can be made into a firm mat (100, 101).

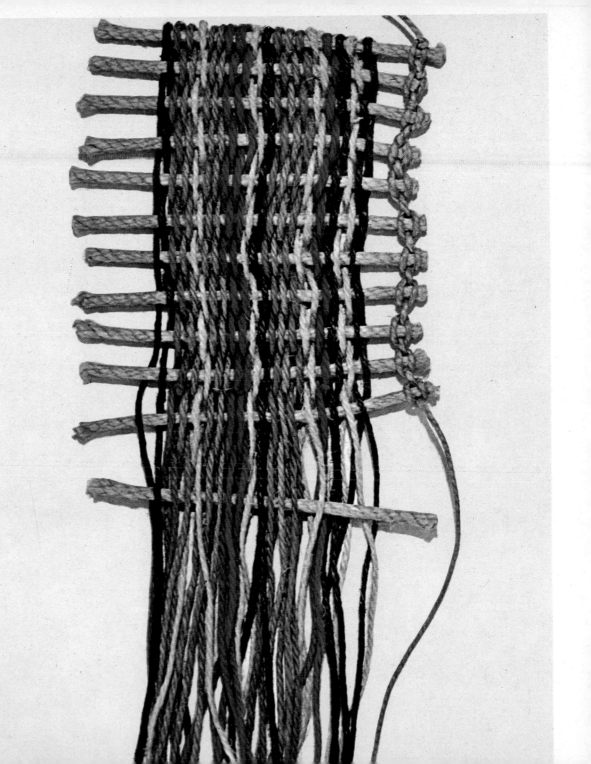

III

IV

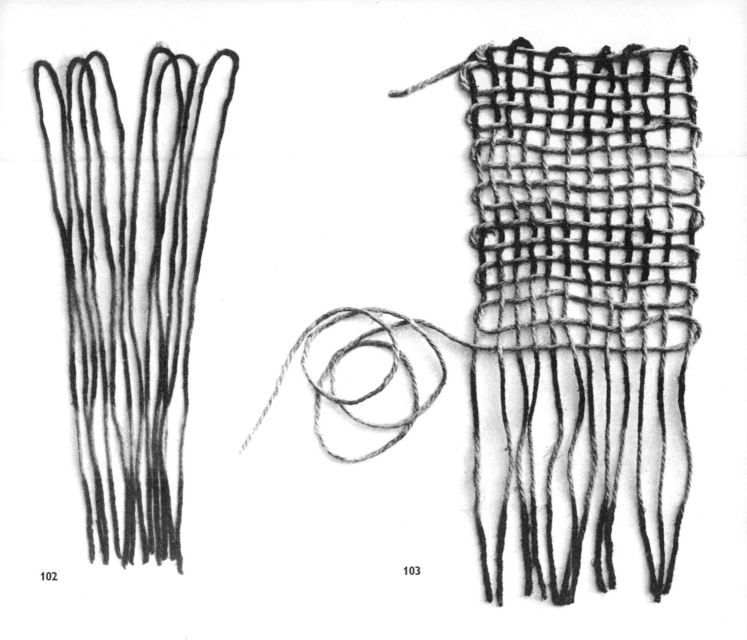

102

103

In this loose hempen weave (103), the vertical and horizontal threads are of equal strength. The vertical threads are partly coloured (102). If the horizontal threads are loosely pulled through, the resulting weave takes on a coloured pattern.

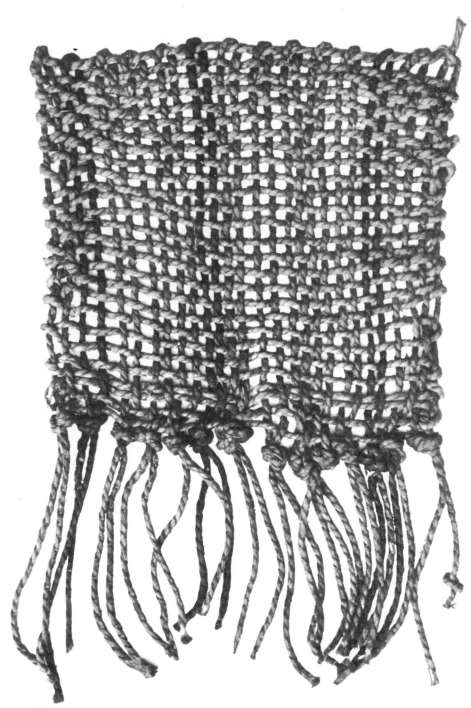

66

104 B 12

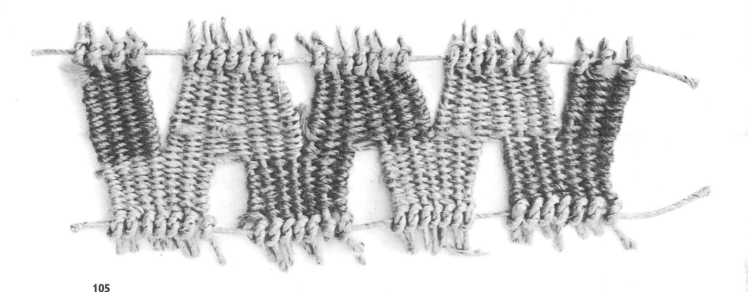

105

The basic form of woven binding is the 'linen-binding'. In this the threads are kept equidistant and are arranged at right-angles to each other. The vertical and horizontal threads are known as the warp and woof threads respectively. In this kind of weaving, in which the hands alone are employed—as distinct from weaving with a frame or a loom—the warp is not stretched. Hence the threads of the warp are as mobile as those of the woof. The wave-like interpenetration in both directions is evident in the piece of string-weaving (104). In Figure 105 the warp threads are knotted onto holding threads. The change in color of the two-colored woof is emphasized by the pushing aside of the warp in this piece of weaving with loopholes.

The loose warp threads can also surround a woof thread with knots during the actual weaving. In the web of knots (107) the rows of knots upon a stronger woof thread form firm ribs with a relief-like effect. Such a product can only be made by hand-weaving without tools. Figure 106 shows a well-tried method of hanging-in woof threads. See also Plate V, opp. page 80.

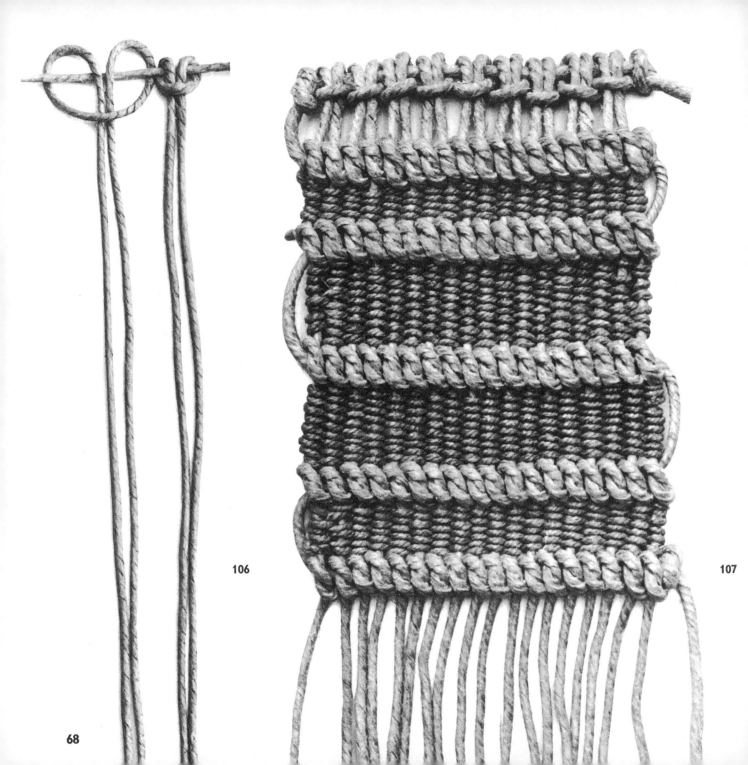

68

106

107

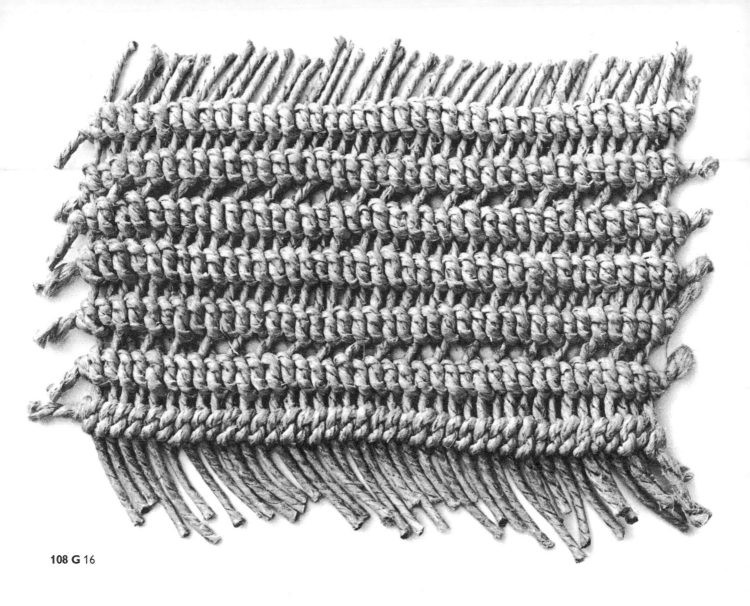

108 G 16

In the knot binding (108) each woof thread is knotted over by the warp thread. A change in the knot binding in the last row concludes the rhythmic pattern.

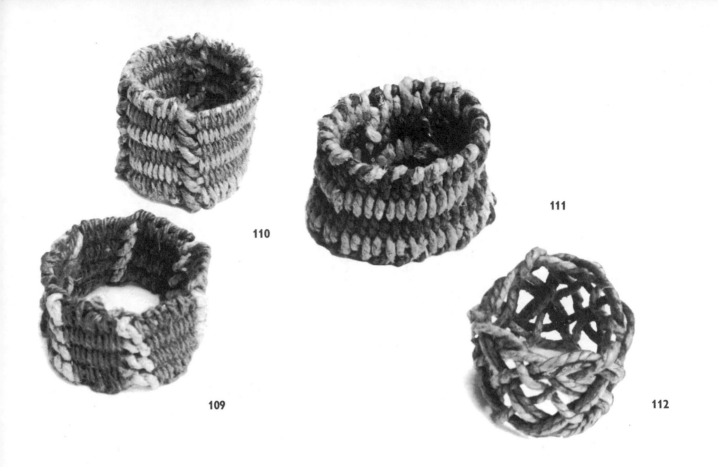

110

111

109

112

The weaving together of hempen threads will be chiefly concerned with the production of small narrow forms (Plate IV, opp. page 65). It is possible to knot them together into stable rings (109, 110, 111). Figures 109 and 110 show rows of knots without a horizontal thread, 111 a two-colored web-band, 112 some loose plaiting.

In the 'string-bag', play with the material has involved a number of processes: knot weaving, loop-chain weaving and coil weaving join together to form a unit (113).

113

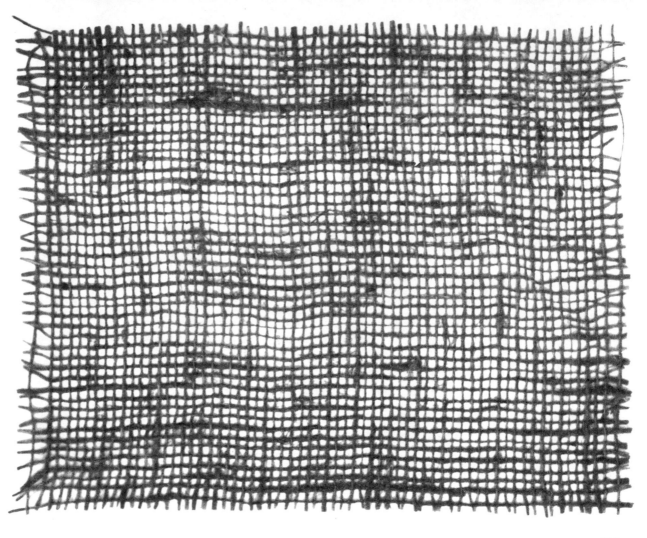

114

The loose jute weave (114) is a useful thing when it is a matter of the shifting of threads or of threads being pulled out. The threads are light and easy to handle and sufficiently loose to change their position. Even when the weave becomes distorted, they adhere to each other sufficiently well owing to their fibrous surface.

72

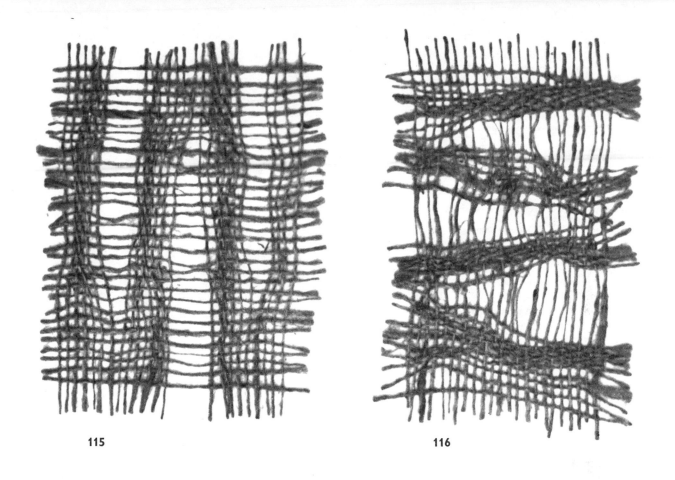

115

116

Without any threads being removed from the loose jute weave, the vertical threads have been pushed out of place in the one case and the horizontal threads in the other. If the vertical warp threads are pressed together (115) the strips remain light. The warp threads of a piece of machine weaving are thinner and more firmly wound than the softer and thicker woof threads. Thus when the woof threads are pushed together, a darker and more opaque strip results.

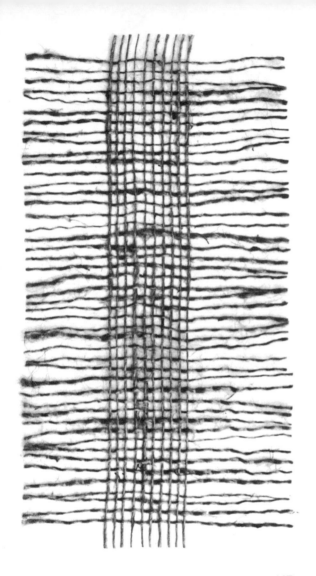

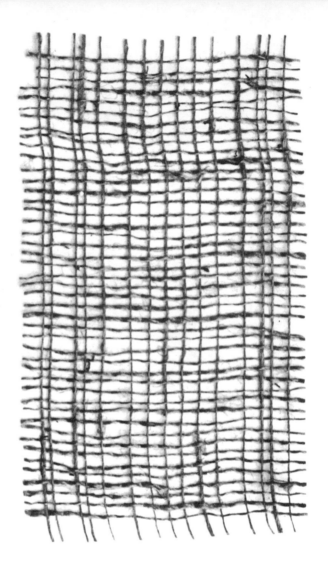

117

118

Jute threads are pulled out from the weave in one direction (117). The vertical strip of weave and the free horizontal threads form a contrast which requires resolution. As the threads are drawn out in both directions, there comes into being a new rhythmical grid effect, while the structure of the weave is preserved (118).

74

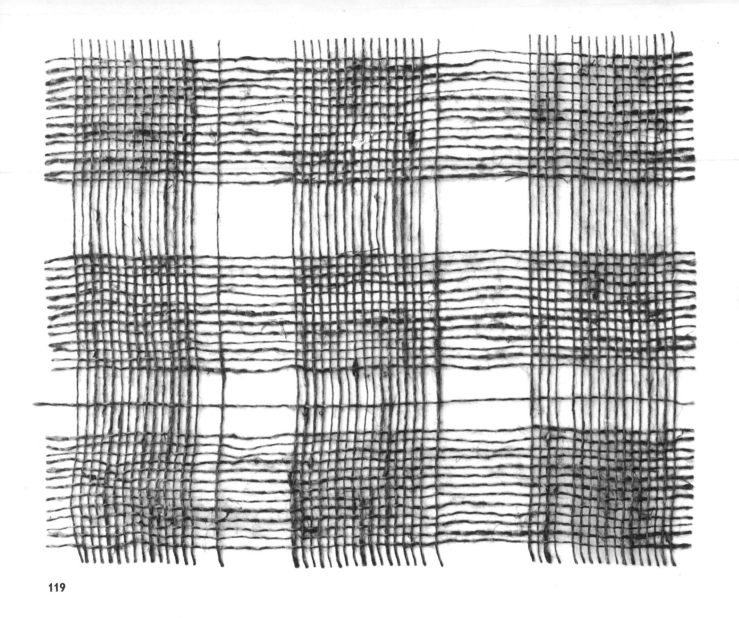

119

When numbers of threads that lie next to each other have been drawn out, groups of threads, both horizontal and vertical, become free. The rectangular arrangement of the linen fastening becomes more visible.

120

A part of the jute weave has been loosened up by drawing out the cross threads. The irregular course of the loose threads contrasts with the character of the whole structure which has been preserved.

Warp threads have been pushed out of place in the loosened weave and this has produced spindle-shaped openings (121). Where the weave has not been loosened, the same treatment produces round openings. The bundles of threads that have been pushed together surround these openings in both directions in flowing lines (122).

121

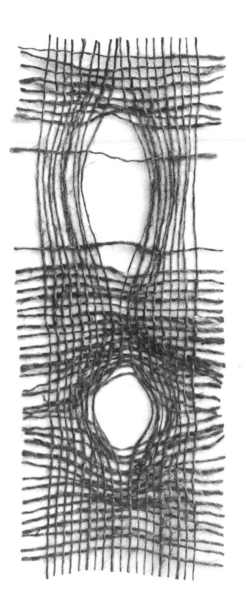

122

123

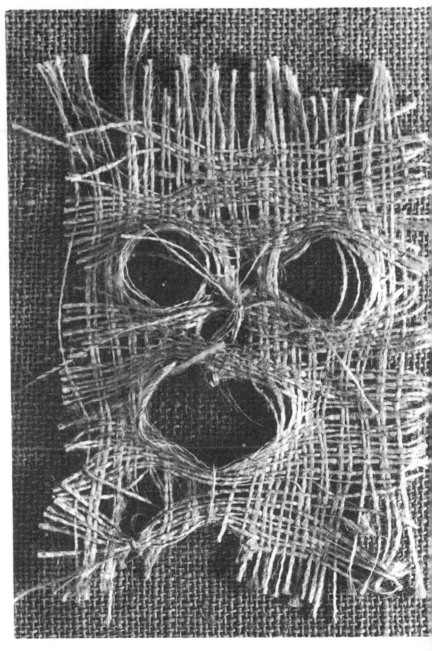

Jute sacking has been bored through with a finger (123). The threads of the weave have been so closely pressed together that the whole ceases to be a plane surface and parts of it project. See also the jute mask (124).

The hollows and convexities that are formed when the weave is pierced are made firm by drawing and tying together the threads.

124 B 16

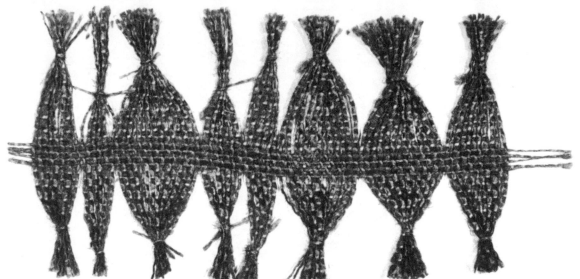

125 B 12

126 B 12

The cross threads have been drawn out of the sacking, except for a narrow strip in the middle. The remaining warp threads have been assembled in bundles of varying width (125, 126). From the strip of jute (127) the greater part of the horizontal threads have been removed and the free vertical threads have been arranged in bundles of varying height. Between the bundles there are now rhomboid gaps which are crossed by a number of horizontal threads. While in 125 and 126 the positive form of the bundles is the element that determines the over-all pattern, in 127 it is the negative form of the gaps that does so.

127 B 16

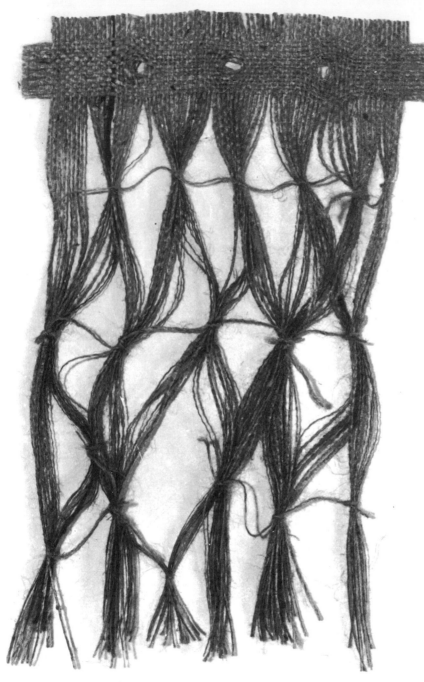

A narrow strip of weave at the upper
end of the sackcloth holds the threads
that hang down (128). The bundles of
thread are partly bound together by
horizontal threads. They enclose
rhomboid gaps of varying size. The
net-like product gives the impression
of unprocessed hempen fibers ad-
hering together.

The warp threads have been fastened
together to make a honeycomb
pattern (129). Light-colored single
threads emphasize the new pattern
with its suggestion of cells.

128 B 12

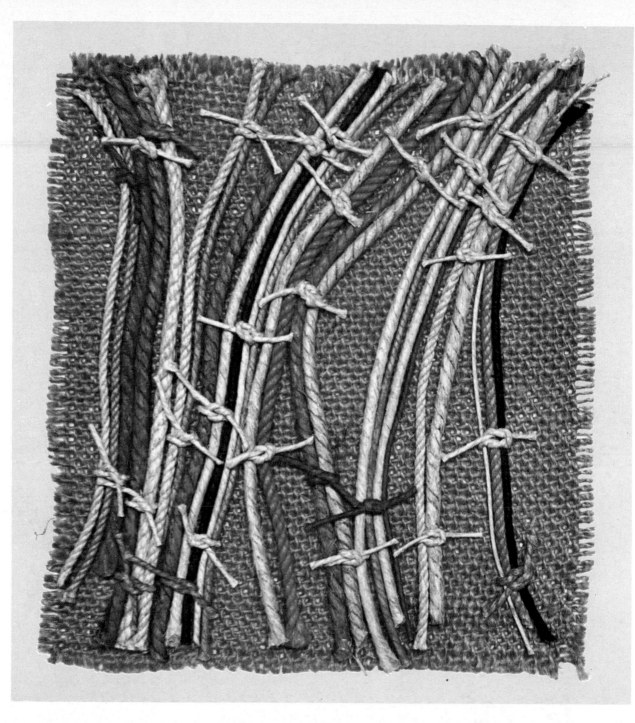

VI

V

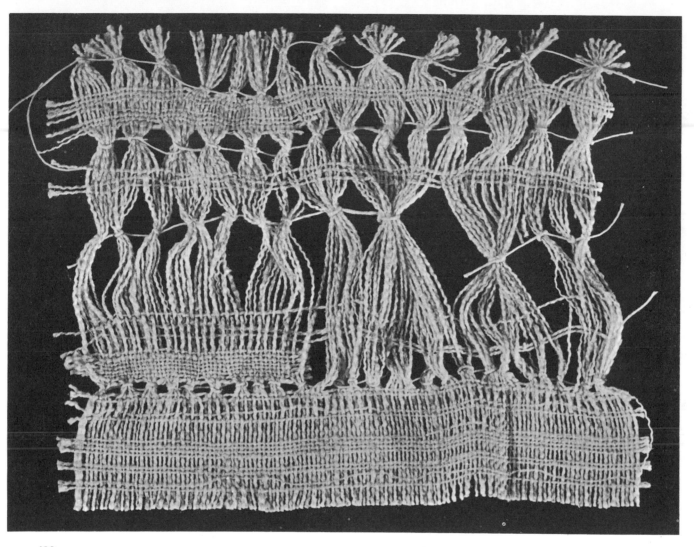

129

Linen is softer and more pliable than jute or sacking. The bundles of thread in a linen weave (129) are more supple. The remaining horizontal threads remain more firmly connected with the vertical ones than in a hempen weave.

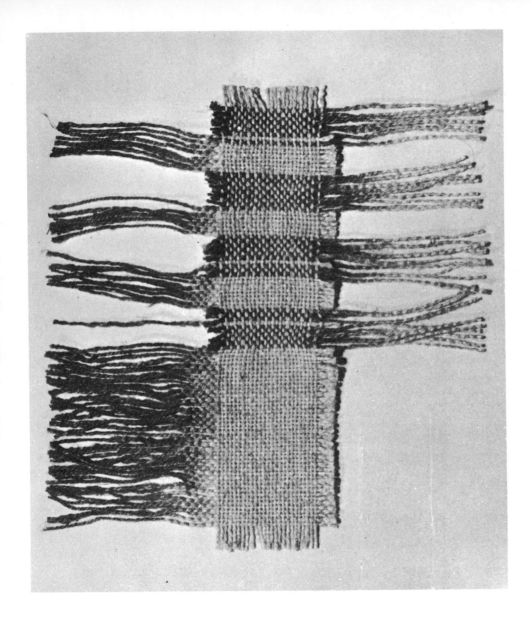

On one side of the linen the warp threads have been removed. The woof threads thus freed have been colored and some of the upper ones have been pulled to the right and drawn into the weave. The result is a colored pattern of stripes.

131 G 17

Colored threads drawn in from two sides.

132

When both warp and woof threads in a weave are drawn together, this causes irregular hollows and convexities (132). When the threads are drawn together more strongly the whole gathers itself into a kind of ball. However, if either the warp threads or the woof threads are pulled tight, folds are formed that run perpendicular to the direction of the the threads. The folds can vary in size and grouping according to the strength exerted in drawing the threads together and the length of the threads. There is a counterplay of small folds with an over-all horizontal effect and a few large boldly-formed vertical folds (133).

86

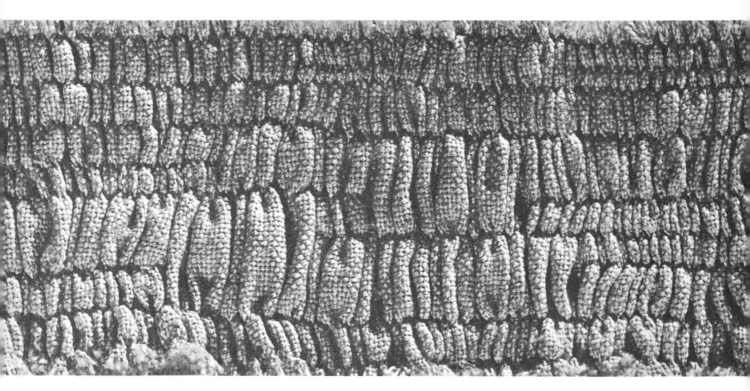

133

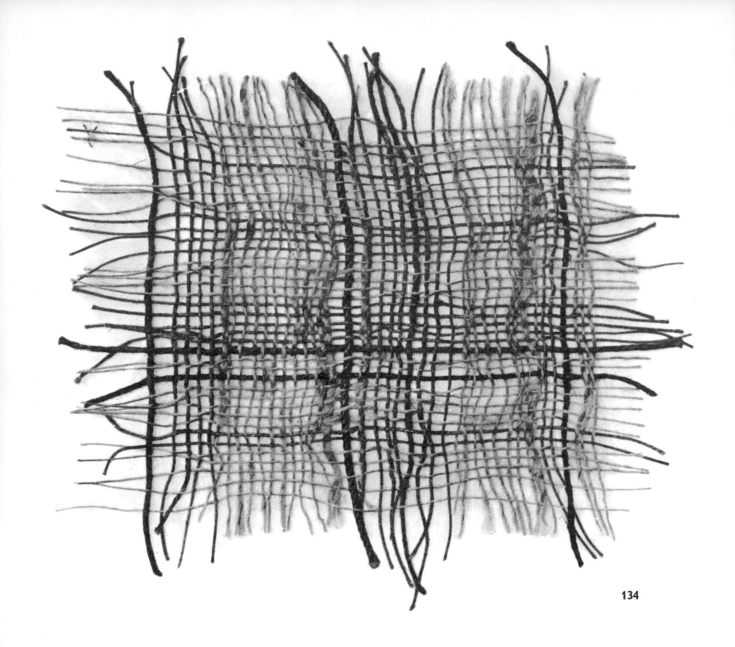

134

Into this loosened hempen weave a number of strong pieces of string are drawn. Their grid effect emphasizes the texture. The borders remain loose.

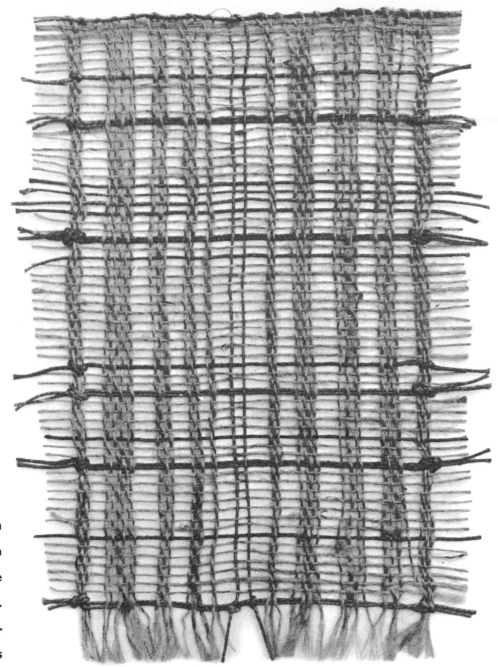

In a hempen weave into which pieces of string have been drawn, the warp threads are pressed together into strips. The pieces of string are knotted together with the threads at the edge.

135

136

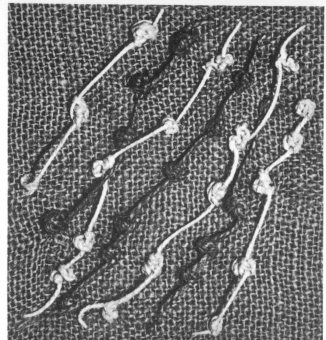

137

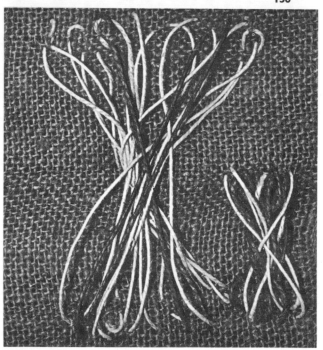

138

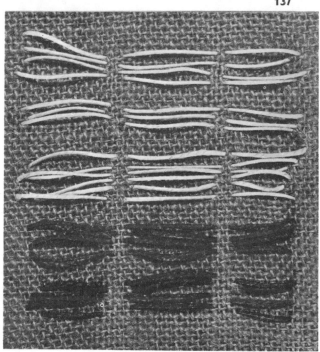

139

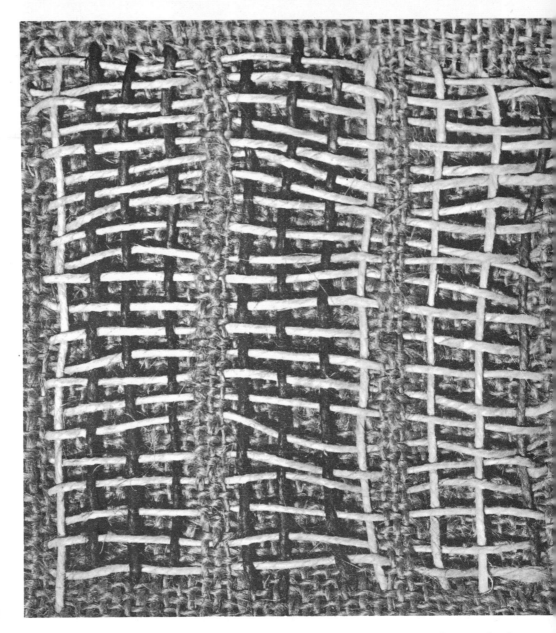

140

Sackcloth is loose enough to allow a piece of string to be drawn through it without using a needle. So we obtain a distribution of knots (136), a combination of knots (137), a thread twist (138), a thread plane (139), and string weaving (140). See also Plate VI, opp. page 81.

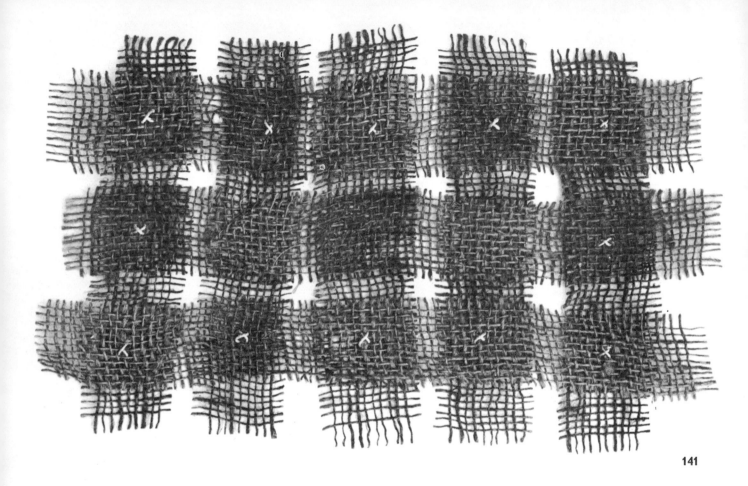

141

The strips of weaving are laid over and under one another—like the threads of a linen weaving—and are tied to one another at the points of crossing (141).

The applied strips are fringed on both sides and then tied so firmly to the basic weave that the thread fringes lie over each other and interpenetrate (142). The edges are thus made indefinite, soft and mobile.

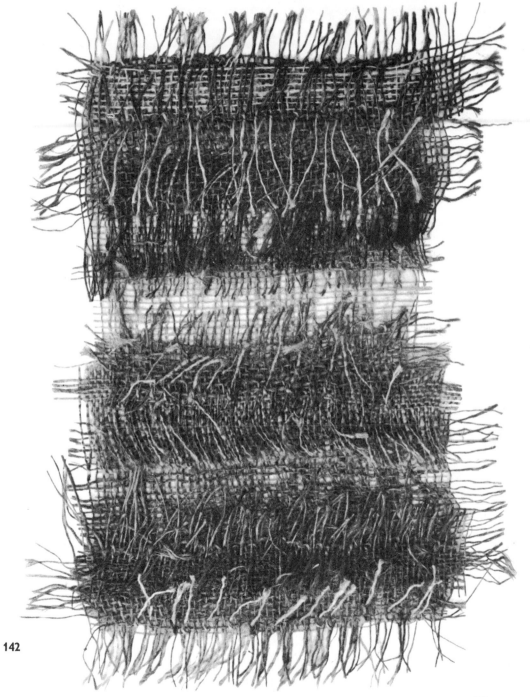

142

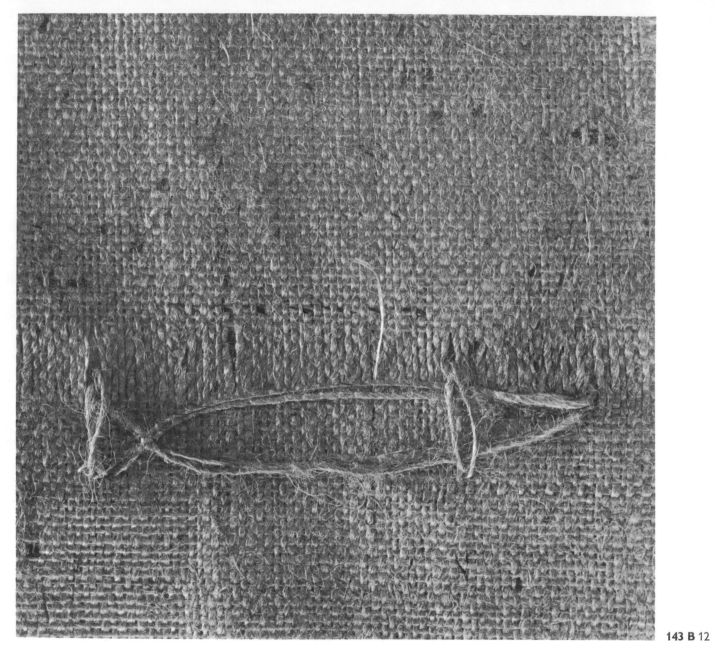

143 B 12

Drawing-out and tying-on threads of the identical weave. The 'thread-fish' (143) emphasizes the horizontal line, the 'thread-man' (144) the vertical line of the weave.

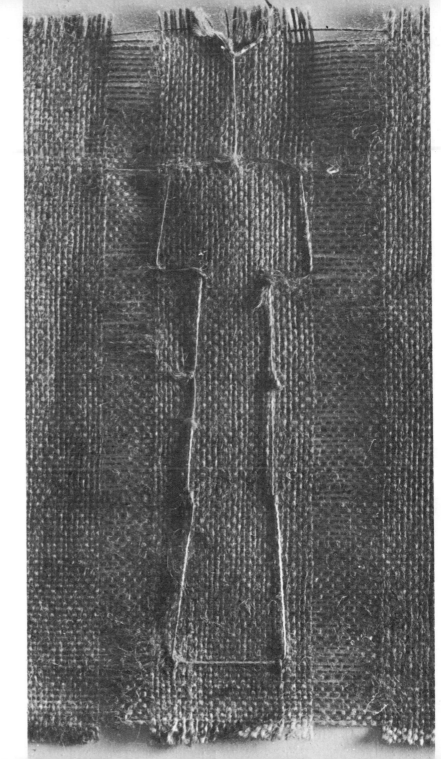

144 B 12

NOTE

Throughout this book, illustrations of work by children and adults occur together. They are arranged according to categories and not according to the different stages of development.

In teaching boys from 12 to 18 years old and girls from 11 to 18, I found that, like adult students, they quickly became familiar with the nature of textile work. The preliminary requirements of craftsmanship are few, and there is a wide scope for self-expression. Also the natural familiarity with thread and weaving produces a lively intensity of work. The material itself, thanks to the ease with which its nature can be understood is an incentive to play, to invention and discovery. It is astonishing to see how all of the numerous textile forms depend basically on a small number of processes with an unlimited number of variations.